The Adventures of the Great Explorers

Story by **Hubert Ben Kemoun**
Factual accounts by **Dominique Joly**
Activities by **Beatrice Garel**

BARRON'S

Contents

Story

Mega-infos

Mega-infos

Game

Stickers

Picture Cards

The Sources of the Zouarn River

Hubert Ben Kemoun

An Old Letter

The pages of this notebook are completely illegible. You can make out, here and there, faint drawings of trees or of plants (unless they are of rocks or of animals), but the humidity has damaged the paper too much for me to be able to decipher these drawings traced in black ink.

Only one letter had remained intact. It was inside an envelope of somewhat stiffer paper. And, because this envelope had slipped into the leather cover of the notebook, the letter was better protected from the jungle weather and humidity. The letter dates from April 1912. The handwriting is regular and very fine, as if the author of these pages had tried to save the little paper he had left.

Mount Sémouël. Tropical Perkie.
April 8, 1912

Jeanne, my love,

I am writing this because I fear that Dilomar, the last of our expedition's porters, will not return. It is already more than two weeks since he left to look for help in the valley. His descent toward the native village of Gaal should have taken him only three or four days of hiking, at most. He would have needed five or six days to come back with other porters to where I am, along the Zouarn River. But time has passed, and Dilomar still has not reappeared. Jeanne, this delay makes me fear the worst.

I buried Professor Van Mudler the day before yesterday, at the foot of a wild papaya tree. On a large, flat stone I carved his name and simply the year, 1912. I do not know the year of his birth. I stayed at his side to watch over him while Dilomar ran to look for help, but my presence here no longer makes any sense. The unknown fever that killed the professor made him delirious for ten days. Now, alas, I know that I made the wrong choice in deciding not to try to take Van Mudler down into the valley when his fever began.

It is another fever that brought me here, dear Jeanne: that of fortune. I am now afraid that it will prove fatal to me. The diamond deposit which, according to legend, is located at the source of the Zouarn River, I will never find. Our expedition is a total failure. We came for treasure, we found hell. I want to leave! I have supplies for only one day, and I am going to try to go down toward Gaal alone. Toward you, too, I hope.

Hell

One day of supplies or one day to live?

Yes, I am in hell, my love! It is dark, because the leaves of the trees are dense and limit the passage of daylight. There is an odor, that of decomposing leaves, that of the spongy, ochre earth that makes each step more exhausting than the last. It resounds with the deafening tumult of the torrent, beating against the rocks. It is also populated by monsters. Here the mosquitoes are the size of tarantulas and the tarantulas the size of a dinner plate. But, above all, snakes rule in this hostile universe. You must be crazy to enter this jungle, yet eight of us did. Six native porters, Van Mudler, and his imbecile of an assistant, who is writing to you today. I dreamed of fortune and glory when I left Brussels and my studies to accompany the professor on this expedition. I promised myself not only to find the diamond deposit with him but—why not—to give my name to a mountain or a waterfall of the Zouarn River, and perhaps give yours to an unknown orchid. Jeanne, I was wrong. It is

not man who chooses, but the jungle that imposes.

After three days of hiking, four of our porters gave us the slip in the middle of the night. To escape, they took our dugout, part of our supplies, and our equipment. But, to our misfortune, they left us our maps and our measuring instruments. "The most important," affirmed Van Mudler. We should have given up. But "Better to die than to abandon the project of a lifetime!" repeated the professor. And I, Jeanne, I thought the same as he did. After all, there were still four of us, we had less equipment to carry, our progress would be quicker, and our goal more easily achieved. I believed it! The following night, after crossing the river south of the torrent and climbing a 100-foot (30-m) cliff, we set up camp in a clearing above the waterfall. In the morning, one porter had disappeared and, with him, one of our best guns. This time, we would have to retrace our steps, but the onset of the professor's fever forced us to wait two days for his recovery. There was no recovery! Each day his condition worsened. At night his groans pierced the jungle and mixed with

the disturbing trembling of the forest. We needed help to transport the sick man across the
falls and the cliff. That is why Dilomar turned
back toward Gaal.

Return!

Jeanne, my only chance of coming back alive is
to try to climb down again myself today. I
know that my chance of succeeding is slim, but
I have awaited Dilomar's return for too long. I
am afraid of death. I am also afraid of the way
in which this jungle can devour me. A wild
beast? A python? A fall and long agony?
Everything is dangerous here. Each step must
be careful, each pause vigilant.

I have not found the source of the Zouarn
River, or the diamond deposit that is hidden at
the top of Mount Sémouël. I think that I am
close, but what does it matter? Others will
return, better equipped, better prepared, and
luckier than we were. Today, my only treasures
are my knife, my gun, and a box of thirty
cartridges. In my bag, I carry Van Mudler's
rough maps, his notes, and enough tobacco for

one pipe. There is also this locket that I continuously open in order to admire your smile. I am going to rest a couple of hours, then start out. I am writing this letter to say that, whatever happens, only my love for you gives me the strength to face this hell in order to leave it. Jeanne, know at least that I finally understand that no country in the world, no treasure, not even a diamond, is worth your love. I will try to return to the kingdom of the living, having as my only precious stone my life to offer you.

Paul Bastogne

The members of the Derida expedition found this letter on October 24, 1938, not far from the skeleton of a man, almost certainly attacked by a tiger. In fact, lying close by was an animal carcass with a bullet in it. It was in the remains of a backpack dating from the turn of the century that the little leather notebook in which the letter was slipped was found. In the backpack, there was also an old compass and a survival knife, both eaten away by rust, a porcelain pipe, and some tattered maps, com-

pletely illegible. Finally, around the neck of the unfortunate man hung a locket containing the half-erased portrait of a young woman.

The body and these few objects were found a half-day's hike from the opening of the underground grotto containing the source of the Zouarn River, much sought after by explorers attempting to uncover its secret. This circular cavern is today known throughout the world for its walls of quartz and mica. In fact, the grotto of the Zouarn River sees daylight only two hours a day, and the play of the light on its walls gives the illusion that it is covered with precious stones. No tourist visiting tropical Perkie should miss such a delight.

En Route

Why do men continue to push beyond the limits of the known world?

Peary

ATLANTIC OCEAN

NORTH AMERICA

PACIFIC OCEAN

Columbus

SOUTH AMERICA

Magellan

STRAITS OF MAGELLAN

The Thirst for Riches

Commerce was the greatest motive for discovery. It was in searching for new routes or rare and expensive products to trade that merchants explored new worlds. In the fifteenth century, Europeans wanted, at all costs, to find a new route to the Far East, the source of silks and spices. What they discovered revolutionized the geography of the world.

In Search of New Lands

As populations increased, some people left their countries of origin to settle elsewhere. On board ships, they set out on expeditions that took them far away. This is how many islands, and occasionally the coasts of new continents, were explored.

to Adventure

■ Bigger and Bigger Empires

To carve out vast empires, generals and their armies left to conquer more and more distant territories. The Greeks and then the Romans of the ancient world imposed their dominions as far as modern-day Afghanistan and the Persian Gulf. In the nineteenth century, Europeans divided up the regions of Africa that they had just explored.

CHINA

Marco Polo

INDIAN
OCEAN

AUSTRALIA

ANTARCTIC OCEAN

Cook

Great Discoverers

—	*ca. 470 B.C.E.: Hanno*
—	*960–1010: Leif Eriksson*
—	*1254–1324: Marco Polo*
—	*1450–1499: Jean Cabot*
—	*1451–1506: Christopher Columbus*
—	*1480–1521: Ferdinand Magellan*
—	*1728–1779: James Cook*
—	*1856–1920: Robert Edwin Peary*
—	*1872–1928: Roald Amundsen*

■ In the Name of Religion

Priests and Christian missionaries made long voyages to convert the people the explorers encountered. In the sixteenth century, the Basque missionary Francis Xavier was the first European to set foot in Japan. Franciscan and Dominican friars covered enormous distances across unknown countries in search of Christian converts.

The Appeal of the Unknown

The taste of adventure, the irresistible desire to go further to explain all the feats . . . It is a need to satisfy this curiosity that excites explorers: sailors, voyagers, conquerors, traders, or great adventurers.

Do Not Lose th

To orient themselves, European voyagers first had to believe in their lucky star. But with time, more and more precise instruments became available.

Astrolabe:
Used beginning in the 13th century to calculate latitude.

Compass

Portolan Chart:
Marine map. It indicates routes and guides ships from port to port.

Dividers:
Makes it possible to calculate the distances on maps and to determine those distances actually traveled.

orth Star

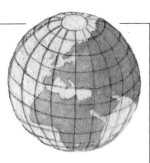

Hourglass

Longitude: *Angular distance of a place in relation to the Greenwich, England, meridian.*

Latitude: *Angular distance of a place in relation to the equator.*

Equator: *Imaginary line at equal distance from the poles.*

Meridian: *Imaginary line perpendicular to the equator joining the two poles.*

Parallel: *Imaginary line parallel to the equator.*

Log: *Float with an attached knotted cord. This makes it possible, with the hourglass, to calculate the speed of a ship, expressed in knots.*

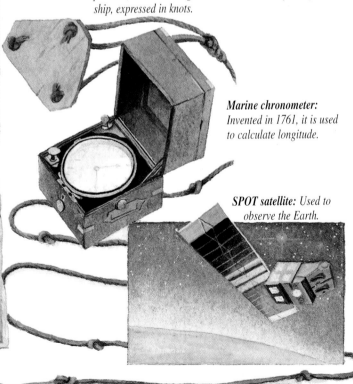

Marine chronometer: *Invented in 1761, it is used to calculate longitude.*

SPOT satellite: *Used to observe the Earth.*

Forgotten Heroes, Failure

■ Forgotten or Questionable Exploits

Most explorations have remained unknown or were forgotten because no one wrote about them. Some were kept secret to prevent rivals from learning about them. Others were depicted in bas-reliefs or paintings, sometimes accompanied by poems and legends. But it is difficult to separate fact from fiction.

■ The Terrible Ordeals of Adventure

Exploits were almost always accompanied by drama, as men came face to face with danger, fear, and isolation. Entire crews died of dysentery, an illness that results in diarrhea; tuberculosis, a disease of the lungs; or scurvy, resulting from a vitamin C deficiency. On land, fevers were also deadly. They were caused by cholera, the bubonic plague, and, especially in Africa, malaria (an illness transmitted by mosquitoes).

■ Hunger and Thirst

In addition to illnesses, there were hunger and thirst, which resulted in death in a majority of cases. One of the survivors of Magellan's expedition (1519–1521) recounts that he was able to survive by drinking stagnant water and eating sawdust, leather, and moldy biscuits.

ragedies

is difficult to reconstruct the
istory of exploration. Along with the
uccessful exploits, how many failures
nd tragedies were there?

■ Failure

oday, exploration goes hand in
and with advanced technology,
ut it does not exclude risk. On January 21, 1986, the
American space shuttle *Challenger* was launched with
even astronauts on board. It exploded in mid-flight,
'3 seconds after launching.

What the Explorer

European explorers brought back food and unknown plants and animals. They also brought back the knowledge of making paper, gunpowder . . .

From America:
Cocoa, tomato, potato, rubber plants, corn, medicinal plants, tobacco, quinine . . .

Beginning in the eighteenth century, botanists used this type of box to transport unknown species of trees and plants during the long months of crossing back to Europe.

Small wooden greenhouses

ought Back

From the Middle East:
Incense and myrrh, peach trees, rice, coffee, sugar, windmills, Arabic numerals, astrolabe, quadrant . . .

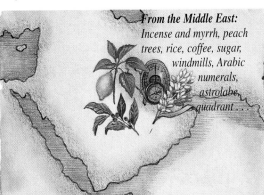

Africa:
hoke, melon, flower, banana ivory, ebony . . .

From the Far East: *Opium, tea, cinnamon, cloves, pepper, nutmeg, ginger, silk, porcelain, compass, gunpowder, paper, paper money . . .*

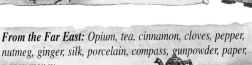

Rattan baskets

From Oceania:
Bougainvillea, eucalyptus, breadfruit tree, hibiscus . . .

First Voyage

On board ships or leading armies, the merchants and conquerors of the ancient world dared to face the unknown.

▪ The First Expedition in History

About 1495 B.C.E., the Egyptian Queen Hatshepsut sent an expedition to the country of Punt, present-day Somalia. A fleet of five ships descended the Red Sea, then reached the turbulent and shark-infested waters of the Indian Ocean. The Egyptians brought back gold, ebony, leopard skins, and trees bearing myrrh, a gum resin burned in Egyptian temples.

First Exploits

Phoenician ships were constructed with moisture-resistant hardwood from Lebanon.

■ The Phoenicians

These merchants traded with all the countries of the Mediterranean. They crossed the Strait of Gibraltar and reached England in search of tin. Around 470 B.C.E, Hanno left Carthage with several ships, traveling along the coast of Africa and perhaps reaching the Gulf of Guinea.

■ Soldiers and Scholars on the March

In 334 B.C.E., Alexander the Great left Greece at the head of an immense army, accompanied by geographers, mathematicians, and astronomers. After battle, they prepared maps of conquered countries and went off to explore them. They went toward the south of Egypt to try to understand the phenomenon of the **floods** of the Nile. They were the first Europeans to sail the Indian Ocean and the Persian Gulf.

❦ *Flood*
A rise in water levels that puts normally dry land under water.

21

Searching for Land

Navigators, too confined in their own countries, depart for adventure and let themselves be carried by the winds and the currents.

◼ Without Maps or Instruments

About 400 C.E., Polynesian peoples reached Easter Island, the furthest point of land Oceania, and settled there. They were guided the wind, the sun, and the stars. They oriented themselves to the coasts by observing the form of the waves and the movement of fish.

◼ The Vikings: Explorers and Plunderers

From the eighth to the eleventh century C.E., these fearsome Scandinavian warriors swept through Europe to pillage cities and monasteries. They also ventured into the North Atlantic and populated lands unknown up to that time: Iceland and Greenland. From there, they embarked on even further expeditions.

o Settle

On Board Sturdy Ships

To cross the ocean, the Vikings used large ships known as "knorrs." Their supple hulls were constructed of boards that overlapped each other like the tiles on a roof. Their masts and their large, square sails could be lowered to form a kind of tent.

The European Discovery of America

Five hundred years before Christopher Columbus, the Vikings under Leif Eriksson reached the North American continent. Leaving Greenland, they landed on the coast of present-day Canada around the year 1000. But it wasn't to be permanent. Attacked by the natives, they were forced to leave.

Activity

The Periscope

Make your own periscope. You can use it to explore your environment and to observe animals without disturbing them.

1. Transfer the pattern to the cardboard and ask an adult to cut it for you.

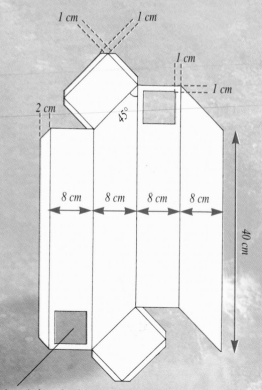

1 cm

1 cm

1 cm

1 cm

2 cm

45°

8 cm *8 cm* *8 cm* *8 cm*

40 cm

viewing window: 6 × 6 cm

Activity

You will need:
- 2 mirrors, 10 cm × 8 cm (4 in. × 3 in.) (You can use mirrors from disposable compacts)
- heavy-weight cardboard
- a matte knife or scissors
- double-faced adhesive tape
- paint

2. Attach the mirrors using the double-faced adhesive tape.

3. Fold the four sides, place the adhesive on the edges, and close the box. Use your imagination to decorate it using the paint.

Now you can see over a wall without being seen!

The Trips of th

From ancient times, solitary voyagers have set off on the road to adventure. They traveled thousands of miles (km) and endured terrible dangers. Thanks to their reports, knowledge about our world became more and more precise.

■ Herodotus: A Greek among the Barbarians

Born in the fifth century B.C.E, this Greek scholar traveled almost all of his life. He marveled at the Egyptian pyramids and followed the salt route through the Libyan desert. North of the Black Sea he discovered a population of nomads on horseback: the Scythians. Upon his return, he drew a map of the world and wrote a book in which he described everything that he had seen.

■ Qang Qien:
A Chinese Ambassador in Central Asia

Qang Qien was one of the first Chinese to cross the borders of his own country. On orders from his emperor, he penetrated deep into Central Asia around 138 B.C.E. There, he explored the routes that linked China, Central Asia, and the Middle East. Soon, merchants would use these routes to transport spices and silk. These would become the "silk routes."

Great Voyagers

■ Xuan Zang: A Chinese Pilgrim in India

In 629 c.e., Xuan Zang traveled the road to India, where his religion—Buddhism—was born. Indefatigable, during sixteen years he covered more than 18,600 miles (30,000 km). Alone, he rode across deserts, crossed the mountains of Kashmir, and went up the Ganges. Upon his return to China, he translated the sacred texts that he had been given in India. He also wrote an account of his incredible voyage.

■ Ibn Battuta: A Muslim Traveler

In the fourteenth century, during a thirty-year period, Ibn Battuta crossed Africa, Asia, and the Far East. He was, by turns, a pilgrim in Arabia, an advisor to the sultan in Delhi, India, and a judge in the Maldive Islands. He knew glory, poverty, and all sorts of misfortune: prison, shipwrecks, ambushes, and kidnapping. In total, he traveled 62,140 miles (100,000 km) and dictated a captivating book, *Travel Journal,* upon his return.

Marco Polo at th

Around 1260, two Venetian merchants, Nicolo and Matteo Polo, began a fabulous voyage. Destination: China.

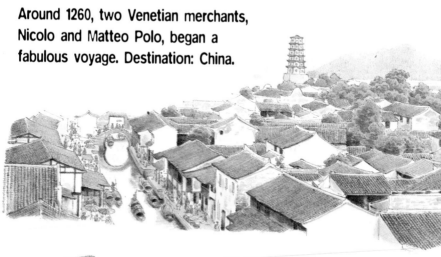

Behind the Great Wall of China

Beginning in the thirteenth century, China was invaded by the Mongols. As a result, this vast empire, cut off from the rest of the world for centuries, was once again open to foreigners. During their first voyage, the Polos were the first Westerners to enter. In 1269, they were received in Peking by the Emperor. They would return to China . . .

Three Venetians in China

During their second voyage, in 1271, the Polos were joined by Nicolo's son, Marco, age 16. To reach Beijing, they followed the silk route, which crossed the burning deserts and icy mountains of Central Asia. At the court, the Emperor Kublai Khan welcomed Marco. He noted his intelligence and almost immediately decided to make him an advisor.

Mongol Court of China

■ Marvels of China

For seventeen years, Marco Polo traveled across China. The richness of the cities, the court with its sumptuous feasts, all dazzled him. He discovered gunpowder, printing characters, paper money, and the use of coal for heat. He also admired the postal system, which used 300,000 horses to carry the mail.

■ Marco Polo: His Story of Life in China

Marco Polo returned to Venice twenty-five years later, in 1295. In 1298, he was taken prisoner by the Genoese in their war against Venice. He dictated his memoirs to his prison mate, Rustichello, a writer. This account of travel, translated into Old French, the literary language of Italy at that time, and entitled *The Description of the World,* was enormously successful.

Vasco de Gama and

In the fifteenth century, the Europeans set out on unknown waters. They wanted at all costs to find a new route to the riches of Africa and the Far East.

■ The Portuguese Open the Route

The Portuguese were the first to explore the South Atlantic. With good seafaring experience behind them, they used reliable instruments such as the compass and the astrolabe and hearty ships called caravels. These sailing ships were easy to maneuver and could come in close to the shore thanks to their low **draft**.

❦ Draft:
The part of a boat that is underwater.

■ The Cape of Good Hope

The Portuguese advanced by small steps along the African coast. In 1446 they reached the Senegal River, and in 1473 Diogo Cao crossed the equator. In 1487, Bartholomeu Dias sailed as far as the southernmost tip of Africa, today called the Cape of Good Hope, but had to turn back when his crew refused to go farther.

Expedition of Vasco de Ga from 1497 to 1499

PORTUGAL

Lisbon

Cape Bojador

Cape Verde Islands

ne Route to the Indies

In the Unknown Ocean

'asco de Gama received the order to continue the route. On July 8, 1497, he left Lisbon with 4 ships and 170 men. n November, the fleet passed the Cape of Good Hope and eaded toward the unknown. In the Indian Ocean it went oward the north, along eastern Africa. From present-day Kenya, an Arab pilot who was familiar with the **monsoon** winds guided the Portuguese to India. On May 28, 1498, he goal was achieved.

> ❦ *Monsoon:*
> *Winds that blow from land to sea for six months, and from the sea to land for the other six months.*

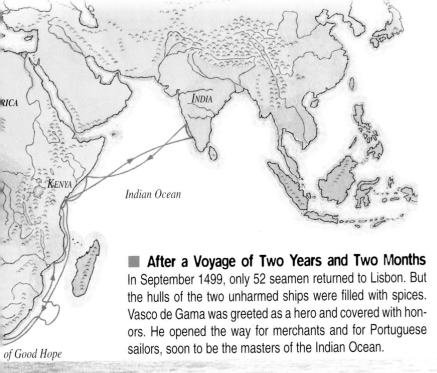

RICA

INDIA

KENYA

Indian Ocean

of Good Hope

After a Voyage of Two Years and Two Months

In September 1499, only 52 seamen returned to Lisbon. But the hulls of the two unharmed ships were filled with spices. Vasco de Gama was greeted as a hero and covered with honors. He opened the way for merchants and for Portuguese sailors, soon to be the masters of the Indian Ocean.

Christopher Columbu

Christopher Columbus had another idea for reaching the Indies, located, according to his calculations, 2,796 miles (4,500 km) from Europe: Sail to the west, across the Atlantic Ocean.

▪ Looking for Financial Help

This Italian navigator defended his plan with passion and stubbornness. At the end of six years, the king and queen of Spain agreed to provide him with money and ships. On August 2, 1492, he finally left on board the *Santa Maria,* followed by two other caravels, the *Pinta* and the *Niña.* On board, they were carrying supplies for fifteen months and fresh water for six months.

n His Way to America

■ On Board, Long Days of Agony

After a stopover in the Canary Islands, Columbus set out for the mid-Atlantic Ocean. The sailors, who were worried, panicked. They wanted to turn around and threatened to throw the captain overboard. To keep them in line, Columbus fooled them by each day noting a distance shorter than that which was traveled. Above all, he promised them land and fabulous riches.

■ Land in Sight!

On October 12, the coast appeared. Columbus came ashore on a beautiful beach bordered with coconut palms. He planted the flag of the kings of Spain. In their name, he took possession of the island, which he called San Salvador. He thought he recognized Cipangu, the Japan described by Marco Polo. In reality, it was one of the islands of the Bahamas, off the coast of the North American continent.

■ The Accidental Discoverer

With the help of natives who served as guides, Columbus "discovered" Cuba, then Haiti. On March 15, 1493, he returned to Spain. In Seville, he paraded down the streets with parrots and natives wearing golden masks. It would be another ten years before anyone realized that he had landed on a new continent. Columbus would never admit it. During his three other voyages, he continued to believe he had reached the Indies.

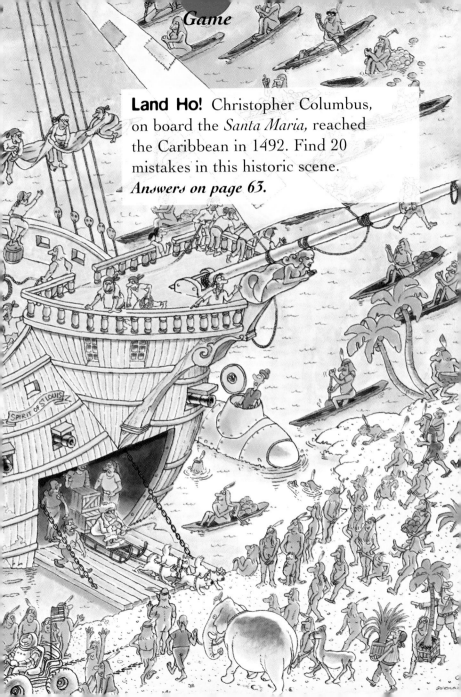

Game

Land Ho! Christopher Columbus, on board the *Santa Maria*, reached the Caribbean in 1492. Find 20 mistakes in this historic scene.
Answers on page 63.

In the Wake o

The exploits of Christopher Columbus excited all of the great European navigators. They lined up to set sail across the Atlantic. What better way to reach the Indies?

■ Toward the Northwest?

This was the idea of John Cabot, an Italia navigator in the service of the king of England. In 149? he set sail from Bristol, England. After 52 days at sea, h arrived at Newfoundland, off the coast of Canada. Next, th Frenchman Jacques Cartier followed in Cabot's footsteps Upon reaching the estuary of the Saint Lawrence River i Canada, he believed he was close to the continent of Asia During a second voyage, in 1535, Cartier sailed upriver an reached the present site of Montreal in Canada

olumbus

Toward the Southwest?

1498, Christopher Columbus landed on the enezuelan coast. Other Spanish explorers folwed him to South America. In 1500, the ortuguese Pedro Cabral sailed to Brazil while the paniard Vincente Pinzón reached the mouth of the Amazon. In 1513, Vasco Núñez de Balboa left on an expedition on foot across the forest of the **Isthmus** of Panama. He discovered a sea, the Pacific Ocean.

Isthmus:
Strip of land separating two bodies of water and connecting two bodies of land.

A New Continent: America

They were all wrong! The lands that these Europeans discovered in turn belonged to a vast landmass situated between Europe and Asia: a New World whose existence had been unknown up to that time. The Italian navigator Amerigo Vespucci was the first to realize it existed. In his honor, the continent that was discovered was called America.

Magellan's Challenge

At the beginning of the sixteenth century, reaching the Indies via the West became an obsession. It would be necessary to circumnavigate the American continent and cross a new ocean. It remained to be done . . .

◼ Preparations

In 1519, the Portuguese explorer Ferdinand Magellan departed with 265 men and 5 large sailing ships provided by the king of Spain. In the holds of the ships were supplies for two years, and a quantity of small gifts—mirrors, bells, and ribbons—to offer to the natives.

◼ Where Is the Passage?

Before reaching the southernmost tip of the American continent, the route seemed interminable. Everything had to be endured: areas without wind, hunger, cold, mutiny, and the shipwreck of one of the vessels. On October 21, 1520, the expedition finally entered the long-hoped-for strait. It was 37 days of hell. In a raging storm, the ships were in danger of sinking at any moment.

Three Months of Agony

The Pacific Ocean proved to be much larger than expected. The crossing took more than three months. The mariners' suffering was terrible. To hunger and thirst was added scurvy. Islands finally appeared on the horizon: first Guam and then the Philippines, where Magellan, caught in an ambush, lost his life.

Eighteen Survivors

Juan Sebastián del Cano completed the voyage on the only ship still intact. On September 6, 1522, almost three years to the day after their departure, he brought eighteen men back with him. The first voyage around the world was completed, proving that the world was round.

In the South Seas

Was there a fifth continent? Beginning in the sixteenth century, navigators explored the Pacific Ocean hoping to solve this mystery.

■ An Immense Body of Land at the Bottom of the Globe

From ancient times, geographers believed that in the southern hemisphere an enormous continent existed that kept the Earth in balance. Following in Magellan's footsteps, navigators went to look for it in the vast Pacific Ocean.

■ Islands by the Thousands but No Continent

The Spaniards and particularly the Dutch accidentally discovered unknown bodies of land in the Pacific. They discovered numerous islands: the Solomon Islands, New Guinea, New Zealand. They came ashore in several places along the Australian coast. But the maps that they drew were too imprecise and none of them showed the existence of the famous **austral** continent.

> ❦ *Austral:*
> *Found in the*
> *southern part*
> *of the globe.*

■ The French Also Participate in the Adventure

Arriving in Tahiti, Louis-Antoine Bougainville believed he was in paradise! In 1767, he took possession of this island in the name of the king of France, although it had been discovered one year earlier by a British navigator. Another French expedition to the South Pacific set out in 1785. Although it was carefully prepared, this exploration turned to tragedy. The ships were smashed on the reefs off the Solomon Islands.

■ James Cook, the Tireless Explorer

This great English navigator was the first to completely
explore the Pacific. During his three voyages, between
1768 and 1779, he methodically followed the coast of New
Zealand and discovered the east coast of Australia. The scholars that accompanied him were amazed by the diversity of plants
and animals. The kangaroos really amazed them! When Cook
came close to Antarctica, a wall of ice prevented him from con-
tinuing his trip. He understood, however, that this was the continent everyone had been looking for.

The Art o

In the days of sailing ships, sailors passed their free time making all kinds of knots. Pieces of old cord were used to make objects that were as beautiful as they were useful. This is how the art of knot tying was born.

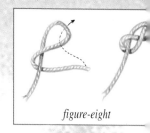

figure-eight

lark's head

You will need:
- a small board, 8 in × 12 in. (20 cm × 30 cm)
- a ball of string
- some glue

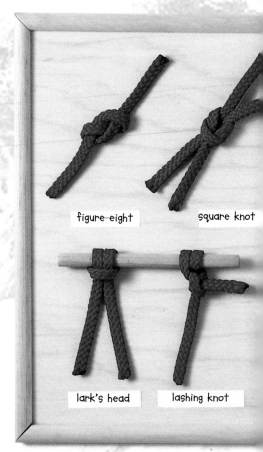

figure-eight

square knot

lark's head

lashing knot

Tables of knots were used to teach young sailors. You can also learn to tie these knots and attach them to a frame.

not Tying

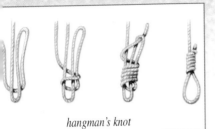

hangman's knot

lashing knot

fisherman's knot

bowline

hangman's knot

erman's knot

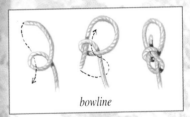

bowline

square knot

Approachin

At the beginning of the sixteenth century, only the coasts of America were known. The rest of the continent remained to be explored: its great size, its inhabitants spread over enormous areas . . .

■ The Gold Rush

Shortly after Columbus, many Spanish colonists embarked for America. Hungry for gold and glory, they penetrated deep into the continent. They explored vast areas and conquered them for their country. With their guns and horses and European diseases to which the natives had no resistance, they made the large native populations submit to their rule. They forced the natives to work on plantations and in the mines.

■ The End of Two Great Empires

In record time, the Spaniards crushed two great empires: the Aztec in Mexico and the Inca in Peru. Their capitals were looted and destroyed. In their places, they founded Mexico City and Lima, cities of the new Spanish colonies. The conquerors imposed the Catholic religion on the people.

■ In the Deserts and on the Rivers

Other expeditions headed toward the Gulf of California, the Grand Canyon, or across the enormous South American forest. In 1540, one Spanish party discovered an immense river that they called the Amazon. Another headed southwest into Chile. In 1682, the Frenchman René-Robert Cavelier de la Salle was the first European to go down the Mississippi.

ๅe New World

▨ Scholars Take Their Turn

In the eighteenth century, scientific curiosity motivated the exploration of the still little-known continent. In 1743, a French naturalist brought back a specimen of **hevea**❦. Between 1799 and 1804, other scientists collected almost 6,000 species of plant. They made many notes, drawings, and sketches of them, and, in this way, added to the knowledge about South America.

❦ *Hevea:*
Tree that secretes
a gum that can be
made into rubber.

Between 1521 and 1532, some Aztecs and Incas were massacred by the Spaniards. More Indians died from new diseases than from battles.

In the Hea

In Asia, areas that were inaccessible or too distant remained unexplored for centuries.

■ The Cossacks in Siberia

In the sixteenth century, a troop of Russian Cossack soldiers left to explore the territories beyond the Ural Mountains. Traveling by sled along the paths of frozen rivers, they reached the Pacific Ocean. Vitus Bering, in the service of the Russian czar, explored Alaska and the Aleutian Islands. Until the beginning of the twentieth century, entire territories of Siberia remained unknown. The construction of the Trans-Siberian Railway (1891–1916) made their exploration possible.

■ Mysterious Tibet

Forbidden to foreigners and isolated deep within the highest mountains of the world, Tibet was an enigma for the Europeans. In 1811, an English missionary was the first to venture there. In 1846, two French clerics arrived almost dead of exhaustion in Lhasa, the capital. In 1924, disguised as a pilgrim, the Frenchwoman Alexandra David-Neel became the first European woman to enter there.

■ In the Jungles of Indochina

In the nineteenth century, the French colonized Indochina. In 1866, the government sent out an expedition to explore the length of the Mekong River, to learn whether it was navigable. Their hopes were quickly dashed. The river is broken up by waterfalls and rapids. Departing from the Mekong, the expedition members crossed China until they reached Shanghai, covering 6,000 miles (9,600 km).

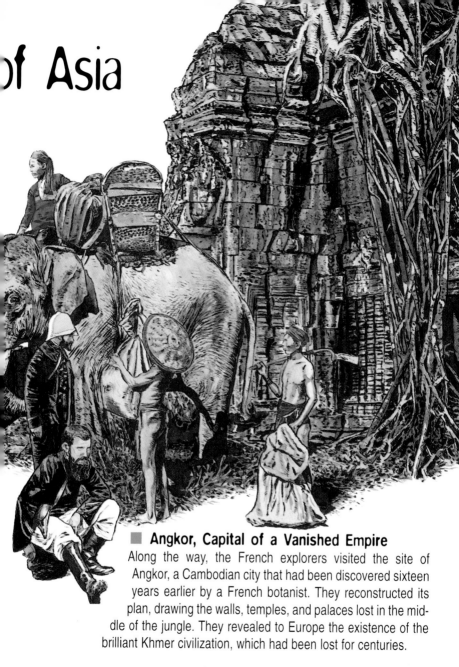

■ Angkor, Capital of a Vanished Empire

Along the way, the French explorers visited the site of
Angkor, a Cambodian city that had been discovered sixteen
years earlier by a French botanist. They reconstructed its
plan, drawing the walls, temples, and palaces lost in the middle of the jungle. They revealed to Europe the existence of the
brilliant Khmer civilization, which had been lost for centuries.

Across Sub-Saharan

Large, empty spaces on the world map. This is how Africa south of the Sahara and Australia appeared in the nineteenth century.

The Mysteries of Africa

Africa was simultaneously a cause of fascination and of fear. The climate, illnesses, wild animals, and frequently warring tribes were all feared. Rivers were the sole means of access into the interior of the continent. But they were very long and difficult to navigate, and their sources were unknown.

Following the Rivers

It took more than thirty years to explore the Niger, which runs through the heart of western Africa. As for the Nile, it remained a mystery for a very long time. In 1862, John Speke found its source in Lake Victoria. David Livingstone was the first European to view the falls of the Zambezi River, naming it for Queen Victoria of Great Britain.

Africa and Australia

■ Stanley Comes to Livingstone's Aid

The journalist Henry Stanley, who had left England at the head of a major expedition, found Livingstone very ill. Stanley continued the exploration of equatorial Africa and the region of Lake Victoria. In 1877, he traveled the last major unexplored river, the Congo, covering 1,000 miles (1,700 km) as far as the Atlantic.

■ Crossing Immense Australia

In 1860, only the southern and eastern coasts of Australia were inhabited. No one had been able to reach the north by means of the interior. In 1860, two explorers tried to reach the interior but died of hunger and thirst on the return trip. In 1880, the extent of the Australian desert was finally learned.

"Dr. Livingstone, I presume?" This famous sentence was spoken by Stanley when he found the lost explorer.

Amazin

A WOMAN AMONG THE CANNIBALS

Between 1893 and 1895, Mary Kingsley, an English explorer, dared to venture alone into equatorial Africa. En route, she encountered a tribe of cannibals, the Fangs. By offering them gifts, including knives, fish hooks, and cloth, she gained their confidence.

THE RETURN OF THE PLUMED SERPENT

For the Aztecs, the greatest god was Quetzalcoatl, the "plumed serpent." He was considered the creator of man, who would reappear at the end of the world. When the Spaniard Hernando Cortés landed in Mexico in 1519, the Aztecs believed that he was their god. In record time, Cortés conquered the powerful empire. The Aztecs resisted but, weakened from an epidemic of smallpox, fell to the Spaniards. Although few in number, the Europeans had the advantage of firearms and horses.

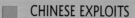

ut True!

CHINESE EXPLOITS

Between 1404 and 1433, the Chinese explorer Xeng Ho made seven voyages of exploration across the Indian and the Pacific Oceans. Commanding a formidable fleet of 317 ships and 27,000 men, he succeeded in reaching India, Arabia, and East Africa seventy years before the Portuguese! This exploit remained unknown for many years as the Chinese did not reveal it until much later. From Africa, they brought back a number of animals to their country, such as the zebra.

SAVED!

From the expedition organized in 1860 to cross the Australian interior, only John King survived. To conquer hunger and thirst, he imitated the Aborigines, who ate wild fruits, seeds, roots, and even lizards, snakes, and insect larvae.

At the Top ar

Beginning in the sixteenth century, hundreds of expeditions had started out on the frozen waters—with as many failures and dashed hopes.

Scott's expedition

■ Land or a Frozen Sea?

In the nineteenth century, all the expeditions to the Great North failed. The men and equipment were not adapted to meet the icy inferno: the intense cold, ice that broke the hulls of ships . . . Around 1880, there was new evidence that the extreme North was not land but a frozen ocean.

■ The Pacific by the Northeast or the Northwest

For two centuries, the greatest navigators desperately tried to find water routes to the North: the Northeast Passage, along the coast of Siberia, and the Northwest Passage, along Canada and Alaska. The first was discovered in 1878 by the Swede Otto Nordenskjold. The second was crossed in 1905 by the Norwegian Roald Amundsen.

ttom of the World

The Race to the North Pole

he Norwegian Fridtjof Nansen allowed his ship to drift
1 the polar ice fields. He succeeded in getting near the
'ole in 1895. Who would be the first to reach it? The
merican Robert E. Peary was the official victor. He affirmed
aving reached it, with the help of the Eskimos, on April 6, 1909. But
rederick Cook, his rival, claimed to have done so a year earlier in
April 1908.

*Amundsen set out on
October 19, 1911,
in quest of the South
Pole.*

At the South Pole: The Great Duel

Antarctica, at the bottom of the world, is an
enormous frozen continent that is even more
hostile. In 1911, two expeditions departed to conquer the South Pole: Amundsen's and Englishman Robert
F. Scott's. Exhausted, Scott arrived at the Pole, where the
flag of his rival had already flown for one month. Amundsen
had reached it on December 14, 1911.

Heroic Adventures

After continents were discovered, new areas, until then inaccessible, were open for exploration.

Hillary and his Sherpa guide, Tenzing Norgay

■ On the Mountains of Fire

At the end of the eighteenth century, scholars began to study volcanoes. Their lives at risk, Dieudonné Dolomieu and Lord William Hamilton climbed Mounts Vesuvius, Etna, and Stromboli in Italy. Since that time, important volcano experts have explored all the world's volcanoes to explain how eruptions occur.

■ The Roof of the World

In 1786, Michel-Gabriel Paccard was the first to climb Mont Blanc, whose elevation is 15,771 feet (4,807 m). More than 150 years later, the highest mountains of the world have been conquered. In 1950, a French expedition, their feet and fingers frozen, reached the top of Annapurna, in Nepal, with an elevation of 26,500 feet (8,070 m). In 1953, the New Zealander Edmund Hillary had to use bottles of oxygen to reach the "roof of the world," Mount Everest, whose elevation is 28,250 feet (8,848 m).

■ The Bowels of the Earth

The Frenchman Edouard-Alfred Martel discovered at the end of the nineteenth century the passage that led to the bottom of a French cave system, the Gouffre de Padirac, and its river, located about 350 feet (100 m) below ground. He thus opened the way for a new science, **speleology**❦.

> ❦ **Speleology**
> *The study of caves, underground rivers, and the plants and animals that are found there.*

■ The Secrets of the Abysses

In the twentieth century, the invention of efficient underwater engines made it possible to explore the bottom of the ocean. The aqualung perfected by Jacques Cousteau in 1943 was revolutionary. Using it, the diver can breathe and move around under water. In 1960, the bathyscaphe explored the Pacific Ocean at a depth of 37,730 feet (11,500 m). This exploit dissipated, in part, the mystery surrounding a little-known world.

The bathyscaphe

Space with

To conquer space and explore the universe: an old dream and an extraordinary challenge to be met.

■ Sputnik 1 in Space

After 1945, formidable advances in science opened the space age. In 1957, a Russian rocket launched the first satellite, Sputnik 1. It revolutionized space exploration. Today, thousands of satellites orbit the Earth. They observe our planet and transmit information from one point on the globe to another.

The Apollo 11 expedition of 1969

■ A Man in Space

1961: a new adventure. On board a space vessel, the Russian Yuri Gagarin orbited the Earth. His voyage lasted only 108 minutes, but he was the first man to travel around the Earth in space. Beginning in 1971, cosmonauts stayed in space stations for weeks and even months—a preview of the space colonies of the twenty-first century!

Rocket-Range

Objective: The Moon

On July 20, 1969, two Americans, Neil Armstrong and Edwin Aldrin, set foot on the Moon. For two hours, they collected rocks, took photos, and installed measuring equipment. After them, ten other Americans also walked on the Moon. In 1971, they explored it on board a vehicle, the Lunar Rover.

In Infinite Space

In the last thirty years, progress has been astounding. The space shuttle, half-rocket, half-plane, was developed to launch satellites and transport people and materials to space stations. Probes have been launched into the far reaches of the solar system in preparation for future interplanetary voyages.

True o

■ **The Vikings were the first Europeans to discover America.**

True. They reached America in the eleventh century, but they were forgotten afterward.

■ **The Phoenicians were the first to explore the Atlantic Ocean.**

■ **The kangaroo exists only in Asia.**

False. They are found only in Australia.

■ **The Chinese invented gunpowder.**

True. They used it first for fireworks.

alse?

"America" comes rom the name of the talian navigator Amerigo Vespucci.

True.

The Portuguese Cabral explored Canada.

False. He explored Brazil. Jacques Cartier explored Canada.

Christopher Columbus discovered America without knowing it.

True. He discovered America by mistake and never admitted that it was a new continent.

The ships used in the Great Explorations were corvettes.

False. They were caravels.

True o

Livingstone found the source of the Nile.

False. It was Speke.

Magellan called the ocean that he discovered the Pacific Ocean because, during his crossing, the sailors did not mutiny.

False. It was because this ocean was very calm.

Yuri Gagarin was the first man to walk on the Moon.

False. It was the Americans Armstrong and Aldrin in 1969. Yuri Gagarin was the first man in space.

The pineapple, ca bean, and tomato co from the Far East.

False. These plants come from America.

alse

■ **The Mekong is a boat.**

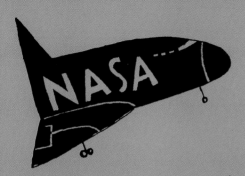

False. It is a river in Asia.

■ **The top of Mount Everest is at an altitude of 28,250 feet (8,848 m).**

True.

■ **The space shuttle is used to launch satellites and to move between the Earth and space stations.**

True. It is also used to make repairs and to transport modules of the international space station Alpha, which is expected to be operational in the year 2002.

■ **The North Pole is located in the center of a frozen ocean.**

True.

Index

Answers to the puzzle on pages 34–35.

You should have found: a flag, a pair of binoculars (first binoculars were used around 1600), a sailor in a modern-day uniform, a missile, an umbrella (first folding umbrella: 1710), Marco Polo eating spaghetti, sailors' hats with red pom-poms, an inflatable boat, Livingstone in a sedan chair, the name of the ship (Spirit of Saint Louis: the name of the plane Charles Lindbergh used for the first non-stop transatlantic flight in 1927), radar, a cannon (1917), slaves in the hull, an astronaut in a Lunar Rover, Amundsen and his sled, the bow of the ship constructed like a car ferry, a bathyscaphe (1948), an elephant, a llama, and a pair of sunglasses.

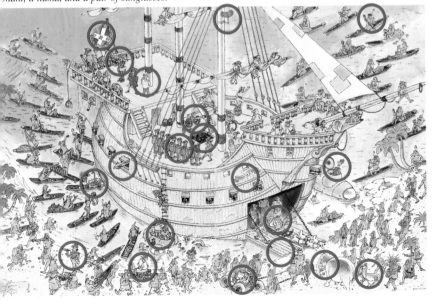

Photo Credits for Stickers

Illustrations

©1998 by Editions Nathan, Paris France
The title of the French edition is *L'aventure des grands explorateurs*. Published by Les Editions Nathan, Paris.

English translation © Copyright 1999 by Barron's Educational Series, Inc.

All inquiries should be addressed to:
Barron's Educational Series, Inc.
250 Wireless Boulevard
Hauppauge, New York 11788
http://www.barronseduc.com

Library of Congress Catalog Card No.: 98-74449
International Standard Book No.: 0-7641-5182-7

Printed in Italy
9 8 7 6 5 4 3 2 1

Stickers

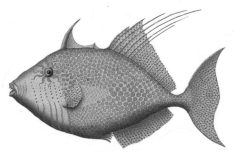

Bource fish from the Pacific Ocean

Inca Sun God

Cacoa plant brought back
from America

Aztec divinity, man-bird,
13th–15th century

Dugout from Ambone,
Indonesia

Captain Cook's observatory

Masked man from the
Sandwich Islands (now
Hawaii); engraving made
during Cook's third
Pacific Ocean voyage

Stickers

Aztec sacrificial
knifes

15th–century
astrolabe

Pineapples brought
back from America

Blaeu's globe,
17th century

Portraits of natives, 1820

Native of Oceania,
1844 painting

Rhinoceros,
16th–century watercolor

Titles in the Megascope series:

The Adventures of the Great Explorers

Amazing Nature

Brilliant and Crazy Inventions

Infinite Space

Life in the Middle Ages

Mysteries, True and False

Our Planet Earth

The Pharaohs of Ancient Egypt

Searching for Human Origins

Understanding the Human Body

Barron's Educational Series, Inc.
250 Wireless Blvd., Hauppauge, NY 11788